DIGITAL CITIZENSHIP AND YOU™

WITHDRAWN

DIGITAL IDENTITY
YOUR REPUTATION ONLINE

MARY-LANE KAMBERG

Rosen
YA™

New York

For Trent and Julia Ladewig

Published in 2019 by The Rosen Publishing Group, Inc.
29 East 21st Street, New York, NY 10010

Copyright © 2019 by The Rosen Publishing Group, Inc.

First Edition

Library of Congress Cataloging-in-Publication Data

Names: Kamberg, Mary-Lane, 1948– author.
Title: Digital identity : your reputation online / Mary-Lane Kamberg.
Description: First edition. | New York : Rosen Publishing, 2019 | Series: Digital citizenship and you | Includes bibliographical references and index. | Audience: Grades 7–12.
Identifiers: LCCN 2018021555| ISBN 9781508184607 (library bound) | ISBN 9781508184591 (pbk.)
Subjects: LCSH: Internet and teenagers—Juvenile literature. | Privacy—Juvenile literature. | Data protection—Juvenile literature. | Online etiquette—Juvenile literature. | Online identities—Juvenile literature.
Classification: LCC HQ799.2.I5 .K36 2019 | DDC 004.67/80835—dc23
LC record available at https://lccn.loc.gov/2018021555

Manufactured in the United States of America

CONTENTS

INTRODUCTION

Future employers, advertisers, politicians, and cyber criminals want you! And they want to know as much personal information about you as possible. They may want to decide whether to hire you, get you to buy their products, vote for them, or use your identity for fraud and other illegal purposes. An enormous amount of data about you is remarkably easy to find online. Some you may want to share. Other information you'd rather keep private.

Global digital citizens live in an interconnected, virtual world where privacy seems increasingly outdated as a concept. In terms of online identity, much of what they do, like, buy, and browse is easily discoverable. The incentives to get that data, analyze it, and use it for various purposes are powerful.

The global market for personal identification information totaled $8.7 billion (USD) in 2016, according to a market report by Smithers Pira, a consulting and testing company. The report predicts the value of the identification market to grow to $9.7 billion by 2021, with more than 60 percent of the demand centered in Asia. A different forecast from Research and Markets predicts such growth to increase to $14.8 billion in the same time period.

Not everyone who wants your information has entirely negative intentions. However, if identity thieves get

Logging in online takes you into a worldwide community. Like any community, the internet requires its members to take safety measures to protect themselves.

hold of it, they can damage your reputation, steal your money, commit crimes in your name, and more. That's why creating and managing your digital identity are so important. You need to ensure that your social network communication and other online activities are positive and safe.

Digital citizens must learn how to manage their personal information and maintain as much privacy and security as possible. It is imperative they learn the elements of their digital identities and why safeguarding these is important. They should also become familiar with various federal and state laws and regulations intended to protect them.

Your own actions contribute to your online data, so you can affect what others who search for you see. You can create an accurate, positive portrayal of yourself, as well as your experiences, attitudes, and personality. You can also remove negative and inaccurate information. However, you can never be entirely sure that anything you delete is actually or permanently erased. There is a common understanding that whatever is on the web, forever stays on the web, in one form or another. Still you can do your best to remove digital "dirt."

Corporations, governments, and others are constantly rolling out new security features for users and clients—ones that will hopefully prevent bad actors from impersonating people to gain access to their finances and other sensitive data and information. These methods include multiple authentication processes, the use of measurements of physical traits, and other techniques.

Finally, you'll learn steps you can take (and avoid) to keep your identity safe. These include common-sense measures that do not require much technical expertise. Nevertheless, learning about how information gathering works can help you protect yourself that much more effectively.

CHAPTER ONE

WHO ARE YOU?

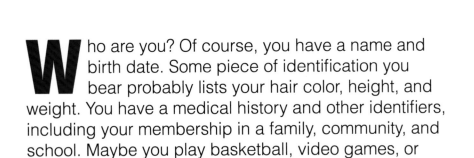

Who are you? Of course, you have a name and birth date. Some piece of identification you bear probably lists your hair color, height, and weight. You have a medical history and other identifiers, including your membership in a family, community, and school. Maybe you play basketball, video games, or the saxophone. In short, you have lots of identifiers that tell people who you are.

Identity plays a major role in everyone's everyday life, including one's participation in various activities. Sometimes you must prove who you are and what qualifications you have. If a police officer stops you for speeding, you'll have to show your driver's license. If you belong to a fitness center, you'll have to show a membership card. And if you want to enter a foreign country, you'll have to show a passport.

To obtain documents, applicants need to be able to prove their identity. For example, only applicants who are the legal age can get a driver's license. To get a passport, a citizen must show proof of that citizenship.

Digital citizens must think of their digital security as something to protect, like they would a wallet full of money, credit and debit cards, and other valuable items.

WHAT IS DIGITAL IDENTITY?

The same is true online. Anyone who has ever connected to the internet has some kind of digital identity, however limited. It is the sum of information about an individual that is available online. It is often connected to one's email address and any URLs or domain names used, and may include such data as first and last name, residential address, email address, telephone number, and Social Security number. But that's not all.

An online identity is slowly but automatically created by online activities, including such information as which websites one visits, games one plays, and one's online purchases, banking transactions, and usernames and passwords.

Digital identity also consists of things internet users reveal about themselves and what others say about them on social media. The more information available about you, the stronger your digital identity. And the more you do online, the more data that is out there for parties to vacuum up. Individuals have digital identities. So do organizations, businesses, and even electronic devices.

One colloquial term for digital identity is data shadow. A data shadow is the total of all traces of someone's online activities. When people send an email, update a Facebook profile, surf the web, or get cash from an ATM, for example, they leave small pieces of information behind. This information may also include places they visit, including tracking of their movements via a mobile Global Positioning System (GPS), enabled on many personal digital devices. All of this data presents a host of potential security problems. As Daniel Solove, professor of law at the George Washington University Law School, said in an article on Infogram.com, "At some point in your life, you're probably going to get googled, and the information that pulls up might affect what others think of you. The more we're online, the more likely the details about our lives will slip out into cyberspace."

Controlling who has access to someone's data shadow is difficult. So is controlling what they think of what they learn and what they do about it. For instance,

Seemingly endless numbers of internet servers power the networks that people use to connect, do business, and otherwise go about their lives. That can add up to a great deal of vulnerable data.

employers have fired employees and decided against hiring job applicants based on what the employers find out about both online. Posts on social media might reflect poorly on the individual doing them. However, many employers think bad behavior by employees also reflects poorly on their businesses.

WHY IS DIGITAL IDENTITY IMPORTANT?

Digital identity protects privacy and security. Computer systems use it to represent the person, organization, or device. That's why digital identity is "one of the most significant technology trends on the planet," according to the website for Gemalto, a digital security company.

According to "A Blueprint for Digital Identity," a report by the World Economic Forum:

> In an increasingly borderless and digital world, privacy and security cannot be ensured through the construction of walls around sensitive information. Identity is the new frontier of privacy and security, where the very nature of entities is what allows them to complete some transactions but be denied from completing others.

For example, you must prove who you are online to log in to social media, shop online, and access a bank account.

BROWSING BEHAVIOR

Our online behavior directly affects the advertising we see on our computers, mobile phones, or tablet screens. For example, imagine that you visit several websites about another country to get information for a social studies report. Don't be surprised the next time you connect to the internet if you see ads for cruises, hotel packages, or airlines that serve that country. If you visit online retailers looking for a new laptop, you'll likely be bombarded by ads for computer electronics, including the very same product you originally looked up, even if you already purchased it.

Such ads are part of a marketing tactic known as behavioral advertising or behavioral targeting. It's a type of marketing based on information about consumers collected from browsing behavior. The straightforward logic here is that a person's likes, wants, and needs are easily discovered by analyzing their surfing.

The information is partly collected through placing cookies on users' computers. A cookie is a permanent or temporary text file sent by a website's web server to a web browser on the user's computer.

Taking the next step, advertisers target consumers likely to be interested in their products and services. The advertisers may also collect users' internet service provider (IP) addresses that identify the computer accessing the website. Sometimes businesses want to know the user's location in order to target them for sales in that area, or to get a big picture of what people in particular areas are buying or looking at.

Behavioral advertising yields better results than other online ads. It offers users exposure to products and services individualized for them. According to a survey by the Network Advertising Initiative, it's 4 percent more successful than nontargeted ads.

THERE OUGHTA BE A LAW

Internet technologies continue to develop rapidly. Unfortunately, user protections in the form of legislation and other regulation lag woefully behind. The ability to collect, compile, and analyze online information can grow faster than the ability of regulators, lawmakers, and law enforcement to respond to it. However, some data privacy laws do exist. More are being considered.

As of July 2017 in the United States, no single federal law focused on collecting and using personal data. However, several federal laws offer user protections concerning the collection and use of personal data.. These laws deal with such topics as privacy, financial data, health information and medical records, electronic communication, and use of personal details in advertising, marketing, and deceptive practices.

In addition to federal legislation, many states have laws that govern online privacy. California, for example, has passed numerous measures—unsurprising, since many online tech companies are headquartered in the state. The California Civil Code was the first security breach notification state law in the United States. It required individuals and businesses that own or license computerized data to tell all state residents affected if its system was breached. Many other state legislatures enacted similar laws following California's example. Some of them concern responses to security breaches. Others include requirements to avoid breaches in the first place. The California Electronic Communications Privacy Act restricts law enforcement agencies that want to obtain someone's electronic communication as part of their investigations.

Along with federal and state laws, government agencies have imposed regulations about the use and sharing of digital identities. So have such industry groups as mobile marketing and online advertising

The amount of profit to be made off people's data and identity is tremendous, and attracts all kinds of unsavory characters.

FEDERAL LAWS PROTECT DIGITAL INTEGRITY

Several federal laws regulate issues concerning digital identity. Among the most important are the following:

- The Federal Trade Commission Act covers unfair practices in the use of online privacy and data security.
- The Children's Online Privacy Protection Act regulates collection of information from children.
- The Financial Services Modernization Act, also known as the Gramm-Leach-Bliley Act, protects individuals' financial information. It applies to the use of personal data by banks, securities firms, and insurance companies. In some cases, it makes financial institutions give their customers notice of privacy policies and give individuals the chance to opt out of information-sharing policies.
- The Health Insurance Portability and Accountability Act concerns the collection and electronic transmission of medical records. It applies to health care providers, pharmacies, data processors, and others who have access to an individual's health information. One part of the law requires organizations to notify anyone whose protected medical data has been breached. A data breach is an intentional or unintentional incident where confidential information is released, viewed, or stolen by an unauthorized entity. A data breach is also called unintentional information disclosure, data leak, and data spill.

(continued on the next page)

(continued from the previous page)

- **The Fair Credit Reporting Act regulates lenders and credit card companies that report on consumers' credit histories and other factors that lenders and insurance companies use to determine a person's eligibility for services.**
- **The Electronic Communications Privacy Act covers secretly receiving electronic communication directed elsewhere.**
- **The Computer Fraud and Abuse Act applies to computer tampering.**
- **The CAN-SPAM Act requires businesses that send commercial email messages to include a way for the recipient to opt out of receiving further ads from the sender.**

companies. For instance, the advertising industry's guidelines recommend that behavioral advertisers use an icon on their websites. The icon links to a page where someone can learn about the company's data collection policies and opt out of at least some of the advertiser's online tracking.

Although many such rules lack the force of law, a series of them have helped create self-regulatory guidelines for companies known as best practices. Best practices are guidelines that have become accepted standards of operation for members of an industry. They result from industry-wide agreement on the best way to do things. In some cases, the recommendations help businesses comply with legal or ethical requirements.

ACTING GLOBALLY

Protecting digital identities is a worldwide affair. The United States is only one of many countries developing data protection regulation. Global businesses must comply with a variety of requirements concerning the collection and management of personal information.

The European Union (EU), for example, has adopted the General Data Protection Regulation (GDPR), which took effect May 25, 2018. The GDPR concerns the export of personal data outside the EU. Its purpose is to unify requirements among all member countries in order

One's Social Security number is among the the most sensitive bits of private information that can be all too easily uncovered by bad actors digging around online.

to simplify legal issues for international businesses. The GDPR includes a list of digital rights that return control of personal data to citizens and residents.

In Canada, the Personal Information Protection and Electronic Documents Act (PIPEDA) complies with the EU law. Like the European regulation, it recognizes individuals' right of privacy. The Canadian law defines personal information as data about an identifiable individual. The PIPEDA requires an organization to get consent from a person before it collects, uses, or discloses personal information. It must also use lawful methods to collect data and establish reasonable policies for collecting data and ensuring privacy.

CHAPTER TWO

UNDER CONSTRUCTION

Your own actions contribute to form your digital identity. These actions include choosing usernames and passwords to log in at particular sites. It also involves figuring out which photos and messages to post on social media. Which websites to visit is also a personal choice that is trackable and visible. All of this data is automatically collected. However, that doesn't mean you're completely at the mercy of shadowy actors online. You can build your own identity in a positive way.

The first step is to search for yourself online. Just enter your name in a search engine. Do several searches using your full name, your name with middle initial, and any nicknames. Start with Google, Yahoo!, and Dogpile. Go to Facebook, Instagram, and other social media sites and do the same thing. You might be surprised what pops up in the search results.

Don't stop there. Enter the several versions of your name followed by the word "image" or "photo," or look them up via a specific portal, like Google Images. Also

Social media networking sites like Facebook scoop up tons of user data. Third parties pay such companies for one's personal details, behavior, likes, and interactions.

do a search for your phone number and email address. Check social media, blogs, and any forums, bulletin boards, or other sites for your old posts and photos.

If nothing yet appears about you, you're in a great position to start from scratch and partly control what you want people to know about you—whether they are prospective employers, future teachers, or potential partners and friends. According to Career Hub, "If you don't exist online, you don't exist . . . or you don't matter." This is not necessarily a bad thing if it is what you prefer. If something does come up, evaluate how it might affect what others think of you. If you have your own website, take a good look at each page or section.

DELETE THE DIGITAL DIRT

The second step is to get rid of as much negative information as you can. We can think of anything undesirable we find as digital dirt. This includes any unflattering or risqué photos or information connected to your name that contributes to a negative online reputation. Objectionable jokes are no-nos. So are negative comments about present or future employers, if you have a vague sense of who they might be.

Digital dirt also includes negative messages you've written in blogs or chat rooms. While it's fine to post your political views and other opinions, be sure what you've written accurately reflects your views. Ask yourself whether your posts are harmful or hurtful to others. Of course, never post anything that incites violence or hatred. Also check for negative or inaccurate information others have posted about you.

Do the best you can to delete any digital dirt you find. If you choose not to take down something questionable, be ready to discuss it if a potential employer asks about it. If you find inaccurate or objectionable photos or information on someone else's website, contact the webmaster and ask that it be corrected or removed.

Remember that anything posted online tends to stay online. Even if you try to delete something, you have no

Beyond the immediate media controversy over Olympic swimming champion Michael Phelps' consumption of marijuana, many stories and posts about it will likely stay online for years to come.

guarantee that it's ever truly gone. Thus, take care whenever you post. This practice is nowhere more important than when you apply for a job. According to Career Masters

OUT WITH THE BAD

Social media websites offer instructions on how to remove photos and messages. Check the websites' help pages for assistance. Here are some instructions from Facebook and Instagram:

To remove a photo from Facebook:

- Click on the photo.
- Click Options on the menu bar below the photo.
- Select Delete This Photo.
- Click Delete.

To hide or delete a post from your Facebook page:

- Click on the top right corner of the post on your page's timeline.
- Select Hide or Delete.

To remove a photo or video from your Instagram Story:

- Open your story
- Tap in the bottom right of the photo or video you'd like to delete
- Tap Delete.

Most sites allow users to adjust their security settings, though some are easier to negotiate than others.

(continued on the next page)

(continued from the previous page)

- Tap again to confirm.

To remove a photo or comment from Instagram:
If you post something, you can delete both your own comments and other people's comments. On other people's posts, you can delete only your own comments.

- Tap the reply balloon below the photo or tap any comment.
- Swipe to the left and over the comment you'd like deleted.
- Tap the delete symbol (it's the phone with the garbage can on it).

Talk, 63 percent of employers questioned had Googled an applicant's name before asking him or her for an interview. Many of these employers rule out potential employers based on what they find.

I'M POSITIVE

The third step in creating and improving your online identity is to place positive photos and information where they are likely to be found. Strategically building a digital identity is a twenty-first century skill. While you might not need to do so, depending on your career goals and interests, be aware that competitors for jobs and other opportunities might, thus putting them at an advantage over you.

One way certain professionals and future professionals get a leg up is by creating a personal brand. A personal brand is a way to market oneself by actively creating the impression you want others to have about you. To form your brand, decide who you want to be. How will you brand yourself? A personal brand is a consistent (and hopefully truthful) way to present yourself to others—both online and offline. This is no place to be humble. Someone's personal brand should reflect the authentic person, including his or her activities, interests, and professional goals and accomplishments.

You should be able to state your personal brand in one or two sentences. For example, a high school boy who wants to become a professional artist also

A professional, well-dressed profile pic projects positivity to those who may be searching your name online.

POSTING A POSITIVE PROFILE

A personal profile should reflect facts about a person's interests, activities, and goals. It should also reflect a sense of the person's personality. Here's an example of a high school student's profile:

I've always been passionate about everything I do. I give my all to whatever activity I participate in. Throughout my childhood, I played baseball and soccer and developed the skills needed to make the high school varsity teams in both sports. In my junior year, our baseball team won the Kansas State Championship. In soccer, I was honored as Kansas State Offensive Player of the Year. In grade school, I started playing the cello and took private lessons. In high school, I earned a spot on the All-State Orchestra.

Throughout all of these activities, my first love has always been art. As a young child I took lessons at the Nelson-Atkins Museum of Art in Kansas City, Missouri. I was a regional finalist in the Doodle for Google art contest during grade school and won a trip to New York City. During summers, I attended local art camps. And as I got older, I took classes at the Kansas City Art Institute. Recently, I've also developed an interest in art history and art museums.

I want to become a professional artist. I might also be interested in a career as a museum curator. My goals are to attend an art school after high school graduation. I plan to put my sports and music activities on hold and devote myself to learning the processes of creating art in all media, as well as immersing myself in the history of art.

plays soccer and the cello and is active in his church. A high school girl who wants to work in advertising and marketing might also be a competitive dancer who has an avid interest in ancient Egypt and works part-time preparing marketing materials for a small business.

Once the personal brand is decided on, it is time to set up electronic profiles. A profile should present a person's "story." How did they get to be who and where they are today? Experts agree that the most effective way to present a profile is to use the first person "I" to give readers a sense of personal closeness with you.

The internet offers numerous places to set up a personal profile. Be selective about which social media you use and which networks you join. Some good examples include such websites as Facebook, Twitter, Instagram, and Pinterest. As you get ready to enter the workforce, post on career-oriented sites like LinkedIn, ZoomInfo, and Women for Hire. Be sure the individuals you connect with share your respectable online attitudes.

BUILD A PORTFOLIO

One's online presence can also include a digital portfolio. A digital portfolio is an electronic collection that demonstrates someone's academic and professional achievements over time. It's a place to organize and showcase work, as well as archive it. An artist, for example, can post examples of similar work they have

A digital portfolio is merely an electronic version of a traditional portfolio like this one, often used by visual artists or other professionals to showcase their work.

done over the years to illustrate their growth. Even after entering the workforce, pros and amateurs alike can continue to show examples of lifelong learning and creativity.

A portfolio should contain examples of the person's best work. Other items include examples of achieving goals and growing both academically and personally. Another important feature is your reflection on your work. These reflections help explain why you've placed different items in the portfolio.

When going digital, use such multimedia tools as text, graphics, audio, and video. For example, you can record oral classroom presentations, trumpet solos, and dramatic performances. One place to look for help producing your portfolio is Wixie.com, a website that is part of Tech4learning. Tech4learning is an educational technology company that produces software and platforms for students.

MAKE CONNECTIONS

Networking is a proven tool when searching for a job. It's also a great way to connect with others for the purpose of learning. You can construct a personal learning network to reach others who share your interests, as well as experts in your field of interest and other resources. A personal learning network is a group of people you choose to interact with for the purpose of learning through exchanging ideas, questions, thoughts, and resources.

The best part is you decide who you want to include in your network. Your learning network provides a way to collect data and share knowledge. You can simply add a "friend" or "follow" someone. Or, you can share your own ideas and comments. As you develop expertise on a subject, share your newfound information. The more you post meaningful, useful content, the more others will want to follow you.

You can also subscribe to Google Alerts to monitor the internet. This will provide links to articles, trends, and other information about the industry, company, or topics you're interested in. Google's search engine looks for new results for your keywords. Then Google Alerts sends you an email to notify you of new web pages, blogs, or research about your topic.

BECOME A BLOGGER

Another way to enhance your digital identity is to create a blog. "Blog" is short for weblog. It's a frequently updated website or webpage where an individual (or business) provides something of interest on the internet. You could think of it as your own personal newspaper column.

You can make it about anything you want. A blog might contain personal comments on current events or a specific topic by the blogger or a guest blogger. Blogs often also include articles, photos, videos, and hyperlinks to other sites with related material.

Once you join the blogosphere, you'll connect with others who share your interests. The blogosphere is the total of all blogs and personal websites on the internet. Link to blogs by other bloggers. Ask them to link to yours.

There are many sites online that host blogs. Some of the more popular ones include Blogger.com, WordPress.com, and LiveJournal.com. You can set up a blog through personal websites as well. As with anything you post online, create clear, interesting content, and remember to use good writing skills, spelling, and grammar.

CHAPTER THREE

ARE YOU WHO YOU SAY YOU ARE?

O ne's online identity in the digital world might be separated among different accounts. You can have different user IDs for different purposes. For example, you can use one for email, another for online shopping, and still another for online banking. (The same goes for different passwords.) If you're just surfing the web, you don't need to prove who you are.

However, many other interactions and services require whole separate accounts and information. For instance, if you want to shop online, see your health records, access a members-only website, or get through a paywall for a news site, the online service needs a way to make sure the user really is you.

Thanks to threats of widespread fraud, identity theft, and data breaches, users need ways to ensure that their internet-based transactions remain private and secure. Online services must protect their users. Many breaches occur through hackers gaining access to users' login information. That's why many organizations use identity authentication measures to

Scam artists will often try to collect enough information about someone to use in order to trick call center employees and other parties into obtaining credit cards, loans, and more.

ensure the identity of users who have connected with or interact with them.

Different types of transactions require different levels of security measures. An important measure is multifactor authentication (MFA). MFA is a security method that requires two or more pieces of information at login. For example, if you want to withdraw money from an automatic teller machine (ATM), or cash machine, you insert your bank card, then enter your personal identification number (PIN). You need to have the physical card on your person, and the PIN to access your account.

FAVORITE FACTORS

Multifactor authentication methods include several choices of traits organizations can choose to include. Organizations choose the ones they want to use, keeping in mind both security issues and ease of use. Here are some available methods:

- Hardware tokens are such small devices as smart cards, key fobs, or a USB instrument that a user plugs in when requested.
- Soft tokens are software applications that send notification to the user's mobile device. If the user requested "entry" into the website, he or she approves the request. If not, he or she declines.
- SMS/text messages are sent to a user's mobile phone with a one-time passcode the user then enters on the login screen of another device.
- Phone calls to users at preapproved phone numbers require the user to correctly answer a voice prompt to gain access.
- Emails to users contain a link the users click on if the authentication is authorized.
- Security questions already recorded in the system are asked of the user and require correct answers.
- Biometric devices are built in to most smartphones for such methods as fingerprint, voice, or facial recognition or other scans.

In some cases, you simply need a user ID and a password. For instance, you can set up a variety of email accounts simply by creating an email address and adding a password. However, other activities require additional measures. In general, business-to-business transactions require stronger security than consumer ones, or peer-to-peer ones. Or, your online service may provide additional security by requiring a username and password, as well as your fingerprint.

TAKING YOUR MEASUREMENTS

If you've ever unlocked an iPhone using your fingerprint for Apple's Touch ID, or looked at an iPhoneX or Samsung Galaxy S9 to unlock the phone with "just a look," you've used a security measure called biometrics. From the Greek *bio*, meaning "life," and *metric*, meaning "to measure," biometrics is the measurement and analysis of a person's unique physical and behavioral traits. It can be used to identify a user and give him or her access to information. In other words, biometrics can authenticate or verify that you are who you say you are.

Biometrics can be physiological or behavioral. Physiological, or physical, characteristics include such traits as the face, voice, and fingerprints. Biometrics can also recognize a person's iris, retina, vein patterns, and DNA. Behavioral characteristics include such traits as a person's gestures, walking gait, and typing patterns. Behavioral verification requires continuous monitoring, rather than a one-time observation.

Biometric verification is growing in popularity in consumer electronics and point-of-sale transactions, as well as security systems for business and public use. Its increased use enhances security and makes transactions more convenient. Users have no need to remember passwords.

A biometric identification system requires a reader or scanning device to record the specific trait in question. It also needs a secure database to store the data. Finally, it needs software to convert the scanned data into digital form and compare scanned data with stored data. The database may be centralized. However, today, once the

Biometric identification systems—like this one that uses one's fingerprint for verification—will likely become popular security features in the coming years.

data is collected, it is cryptographically hashed so the verifying process needs no direct access to the data itself. Cryptographic hashing is the process of transforming a string of characters into a shorter, coded message. Data that has been hashed is easier to find, retrieve, and index than by using the original information.

FAKE IDS

The key to security using biometrics is ensuring that the factors used don't change over time. Fingerprints, for example, stay the same throughout someone's life. That may be why fingerprint recognition was the first widely used trait in mass-market authentication. Blood vessel patterns in the retina also remain the same.

On the other hand, facial features may change as a person ages, suffers illness, or experiences other developments. Someone's voice and other biometric traits might change, even if just slightly. In addition, voice recognition may not work well in a noisy environment. Facial recognition may not work well in low light. Verification systems that rely on those characteristics may be less reliable and less secure.

The use of biometrics is not a 100 percent guarantee of security, of course. Even though your biometrics are unique to you, you can't be confident that your device can't be hacked. As early as 2002, researchers in Japan showed that a hacker could lift a fingerprint from a glossy surface using gelatin and use a copy to fool fingerprint scanners.

Attackers can also defeat other biometric systems. Iris scanning can be defeated using data from a high-resolution photo. In 2015, Jan Krissler, a researcher for the Chaos Computer Club with a screen name "Starbug," demonstrated how to do it. Two years later, Krissler used his method to hack a Samsung Galaxy S8 smartphone. Krissler also used a high-resolution photo of a thumb to fool Apple's Touch ID authentication system. Other researchers used a 3D-printed mask to bypass Apple's Face ID on the iPhone X. Still others unlocked Face ID using children or siblings of the authorized user.

Even though biometric readers are getting more sophisticated, false positives are still a possibility, meaning the

Good passwords and other personal security measures will prove frustrating and unwelcome for those trying to crack someone else's accounts and profiles.

wrong user is recognized. It's also still possible to get false negatives, denying entry to an authorized user. Still, the increasing number of high-quality cameras, microphones, and fingerprint readers in mobile devices suggest that the use of biometrics will increase as well.

HERE, FIDO!

In 2007, PayPal, the online payment broker, had a problem. A plan meant to increase security was mostly ignored by most of its targeted users. PayPal officials Ramesh Kesanupalli and Michael Barrett discussed the need for an industry standard that would support all hardware used to authenticate users' identities.

Six years later, the Fast ID Online (FIDO) Alliance was formed. The alliance is a nonprofit made up of such companies as Google, Microsoft, Bank of America, Mastercard, and Visa, as well as digital device manufacturers, among others. The organization seeks to develop specifications for standardized privacy and security measures that are easy to use.

FIDO has produced sets of rules—called protocols—that apply to the exchange or transmission of data between devices. One is the Universal Authentication Framework (UAF). The UAF is an example of two-factor authentication. It uses both a public key and a private key. The online service registers the user's public key. The user then uses his or her device to add the private key. The private key may be entered as a personal identification number (PIN), fingerprint, selfie, or voice sample created by speaking into a microphone on the device.

DIGITAL IDENTITY SYSTEMS

As the number and complexity of electronic transactions increase, some tech industry experts urge the development of a standardized way to verify digital identities. A digital identity system would make collecting and sharing information easier. It would have to comply with laws and regulations and customer expectations for privacy. Perhaps most important, it would have to include strong protection against hackers, as well as damage, loss, theft, and tampering with identification records.

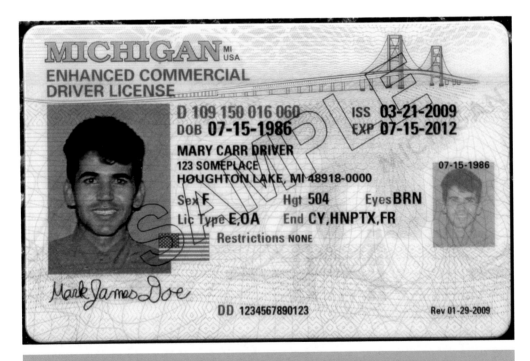

Online identity confirmation systems are inspired by real-world measures to make physical identity theft harder, including enhanced driver's licenses, rolled out in Michigan and nationwide.

A digital identity system includes those asked to prove their identities, those who provide the identity, those who rely on the information, and governing bodies. In the nondigital world, for instance, the identity system for passports uses the same principles. The person asked to prove his or her identity is the one who wants to enter another country. The government of the user's home country provides the identity. The government of the foreign country relies on the document. And international agreements serve as the "governing body." The same structure would be used for a digital system, except storing and exchanging data would occur electronically.

The United States and Canada are working together to develop such a system. In 2017, the US Department of Homeland Security (DHS) awarded an $800,000 (in US dollars) grant to SecureKey and the Digital ID and Authentication Council of Canada to create the infrastructure for a digital identity network. SecureKey is a technology company based in Toronto, Ontario, Canada. The Digital ID and Authentication Council of Canada is a nonprofit group of public and private organizations. It plans to create a national system for users to prove who they are in a private, secure way without the need for a long list of passwords.

ETHICAL ISSUES

While such a system would make transactions easier for both users and organizations they do business with, the idea of a standard, national network poses some risks and ethical issues. Questions posed include who makes decisions, who controls the infrastructure, and whether the huge collection of sensitive personal information is held in a centralized database that may be misused.

For example, an authoritarian government could use the database from the inside for surveillance on certain citizens. The easy-to-access information could be used for human rights abuses. Another consideration is national ID cards. Some countries have them. Some don't. Too, some governments lack the stability to be trusted with such a system.

Or, outsiders could seek to control or break the network. The security required for such a system would pose a tempting target for black hat hackers up to no good. A black hat hacker is a criminal who uses technology skills for criminal purposes, such as stealing money from bank accounts or gaining access to credit card information to sell on the black market or use to buy things for himself or herself. He or she can learn about products in development at private companies or break into government military records and classified information.

CHAPTER FOUR

COMING SOON

As governments, corporations, and other organizations seek a one-size-fits-all identity system, new technology makes one possible. New data storage offers increased privacy, security, and user control. New data transfer methods keep "bad guys" from intercepting and decrypting information. New apps are being developed for using charts, animated video, and other media to show someone's identity. And authentication techniques are improving.

Still, there may never be a single network that serves everyone worldwide. Most users, governments, and businesses want safe, convenient electronic transactions, a way to collect data, and a transparent tracking system. However, identity needs vary by user. So do privacy needs. It's likely

Companies like Google, Facebook, and others generate huge profits from the information they collect and analyze.

that different groups will create their own digital identity systems, work on their own pieces of the puzzle, or develop networks for their own purposes. Some new technologies are already in development.

TRANSACTION TECHNOLOGY

Already in use is a new electronic ledger technology called blockchain. It's a way to share digital data that can be openly (or privately) shared among different users. It links—or chains—blocks of transactions. Computers in the network share the ledger without a central authority. And competitors can safely use it without exposing their own information. In addition, no one entity can tamper with the data.

Blockchain technology creates a permanent record of transactions linked in chronological order. It's the basis of Bitcoin, the worldwide electronic currency first used in 2009. Bitcoin allows encrypted electronic payments from one party to another without the need for a bank or other financial institution.

Blockchain technology is still new, and it's a long way from perfection. There's a chance of undiscovered bugs in the software. Still, the way its components are arranged makes it the most secure system so far. Hacking into it would require hacking every computer on that particular network.

Experts expect acceptance to be slow but steady. However, blockchain technology already is in use in shipping, financial, health care, and energy industries.

Some groups hope to develop a standard version of blockchain. Others are working to create their own variations. Eventually blockchain technology may deliver a lower-cost, more efficient way to share information.

IDENTITY INNOVATIONS

A number of identity-related projects are underway to improve digital identity for everyone. Test projects and newly available applications may soon allow everyone secure, convenient, and private access to online services. A sampling includes a way to access

Digital gatekeepers will replicate similar security encountered in the real world, such as this Transportation Security Administration (TSA) agent checking a woman's boarding pass and identification.

discounts, benefits, and government services; use of electronic driver's licenses; and a way to prevent theft of state tax refunds. These and more may soon be available to the general public on a widespread basis.

ID.me began as Troop ID. It let active and veteran members of the US armed services and their families prove their military affiliation to receive online discounts and benefits, while keeping personal identification or sensitive documents safe from unauthorized view. Eligibility has been extended to first responders, students, and teachers.

Now known as ID.me, the pilot program is being expanded to include the city of Austin, Texas, and the state of Maine. The Texas project seeks to create a citywide plan to demonstrate a model for strong identity verification that can be used in other municipalities. The Maine project seeks to put an identity model into effect that increases access to federal and state benefits.

MOBILE MOTORING

The flashing red and blue lights in your rearview mirror make your heart beat a little faster as you pull to the side of the road. A police officer approaches your window and leans in. The officer asks for your driver's license. Instead of reaching for your wallet, you hand over your mobile phone. It contains a digital driver's license—also called a mobile driver's license. The officer can see your photo, name, address, and date of birth, as well as verify that you are entitled to drive a motor vehicle.

Pilot projects are underway around the world that may soon make this scenario a reality. In 2016, in fact, the US Commerce Department's National Institute of Standards and Technology awarded a $2 million (USD) grant to develop trusted identities based on state-issued digital driver's licenses to Gemalto, an international security company based in Amsterdam, Netherlands. The company ran a two-year pilot program in cooperation with the state governments of Idaho, Colorado, Maryland, Washington, and Wyoming.

Goals for the pilot programs extend beyond verifying driving privileges. Drivers also show their licenses as identification and proof of age for purchase of alcohol and tobacco products, renting a car, checking into a hotel, gaining access to financial accounts, and other uses. So, a digital license must meet these types of needs, too. And it must offer convenience and ease of use for the issuing authorities, as well as consumers, law enforcement officials, and others who accept driver's licenses as proof of age and identity.

To gain government and law enforcement approval and consumer acceptance, a mobile driver's license must be accessible both online and offline. It needs high security that protects personal information throughout its use from the time it's issued until it's used as identification. It must work in different jurisdictions with different issuing and verifying authorities.

Creating an electronic credential that meets these needs remains in its early stages. However, the American

"CAN I HAVE YOUR SOCIAL SECURITY NUMBER, PLEASE?"

There are many people nowadays who have suffered through the nightmare of identity theft, often through someone else making illegal use of their social security numbers. Some concerned citizens have been pushing back against giving out their numbers. Many potential employers, medical providers, and others request a client or candidate's number as a identifier for payment and taxation purposes, while others simply see it as an easy form of identification, and authentication.

However, some people who rightfully fear identity theft and invasion of privacy that the number should only be used what it is meant for: to allow people to contribute to and collect social security benefits when they retire, or otherwise need them—for example, to collect job disability benefits throught the social security system, in some cases.

Some states prohibit employers and others from asking for these sensitive numbers for purposes besides paying out social security benefits. You are well within your rights to refuse to provide this information at any time. Realize, however, that many places will insist on it, and you may miss out on some opportunities and services.

If you are concerned about giving up your number while interviewing for a job, try to talk to the hiring manager or human resources person. Inform them that you will be more than happy to provide the number if you get the job, since you will have to do so to get paid and pay taxes. Be suspicious of any place that wants to use the number if there is no real reason for them to have it. The more places and internal computer systems have your number on file out there, the more vulnerable you will naturally be if hacks occur, and your number can be easily compromised.

Association of Motor Vehicle Administrators has a working group dedicated to determining standards and specifications for such a system. It has produced a proof of concept demonstrating that the idea is able to be carried out. Proof of concept is documented evidence that a product or service can be successful in a real-world environment.

ORDER IN THE COURT

Giving a mobile phone to a law enforcement officer to show a mobile driver's license raises an issue of rights that protect drivers from unreasonable searches and seizures. Once the driver relinquishes a mobile phone to show a driver's license, can the officer then search information stored on the phone?

A 2014 Supreme Court case, *Riley v. California*, would answer that question. The case involved two separate events that carried the same question. The two situations were combined for the Supreme Court case.

In the first case, a police officer stopped David Riley for a traffic violation. In a physical patdown, the police discovered evidence that the driver had ties to a street gang. The police then searched the car and found firearms under the hood. The police took Riley's cell phone and searched it without a warrant. Evidence in the phone placed the device at the scene of a shooting weeks earlier. Police charged him with the crime. He was convicted, but Riley appealed the verdict.

In the other case, police arrested Brima Wurie during a drug bust and took his cell phone. They flipped open

It is important to know your rights when it comes to interactions with law enforcement and the government, online or off.

the phone and saw a number of missed calls from the same number, which had the caller ID "my house." Although they had no warrant to examine the phone's contents, police got a search warrant for the apartment linked to the mobile number. They found drugs, a gun, and cash. Wurie was charged and convicted of distribution of crack cocaine, possession of crack cocaine with intent to distribute, and felony possession of a firearm and ammunition. He, too, appealed the verdict.

After hearing the cases, the Court ruled in favor of both defendants. The law enforcement officers had violated Riley's and Wurie's Fourth Amendment rights against unreasonable searches and seizures. Chief Justice John Roberts wrote, "The answer to the question of what police must do before searching a cell phone seized incident to an arrest is simple—get a warrant."

The ruling (and the Fourth Amendment) assures those who might hesitate to use an electronic license that law enforcement cannot access personal information stored in cell phones without a warrant. The case paves the way for states to put digital driver's licenses into effect in a way the public trusts.

THWARTING THEFT

In 2017, the state of Alabama prevented more than $8.6 million in state tax refund theft on a suspected 37,233 tax returns, according to SecureIDNews.com. The savings resulted from a pilot program of Alabama eID, an electronic identity app. In 2018, the secure service went into full-scale use statewide on a voluntary basis.

Taxpayers download the free app in Apple's App Store or Google Play Store. They verify their identities with a scan of their physical driver's license or state ID. They also provide facial evidence by taking a selfie with their smartphones. This evidence is then compared to data in the state's driver's license database to confirm identity.

Protect yourself if you leave a smartphone in public by password-protecting it, keeping any sensitive data off limits, and logging out of any accounts while they are not in use.

Once the technology verifies that the person is who he or she claims to be, a quick response (QR) code is sent to the taxpayer's phone. A QR code is machine-readable barcode consisting of a two-dimensional arrangement of black-and-white squares that stores the encoded data. The taxpayer logs into the state's website and files his or her tax return. At that point, an alert tells the taxpayer to take a selfie video turning his or her head side-to-side to prove that the image is not a two-dimensional photograph. Alabama was the first state to implement this kind of program. To encourage participation, state officials granted priority processing for refunds owed to taxpayers who used the app to file their returns.

CHAPTER FIVE

WHAT CAN YOU DO?

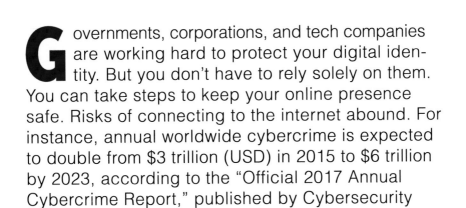

Governments, corporations, and tech companies are working hard to protect your digital identity. But you don't have to rely solely on them. You can take steps to keep your online presence safe. Risks of connecting to the internet abound. For instance, annual worldwide cybercrime is expected to double from $3 trillion (USD) in 2015 to $6 trillion by 2023, according to the "Official 2017 Annual Cybercrime Report," published by Cybersecurity Ventures, an international research and publishing company that covers the global cyber economy.

According to the US Federal Trade Commission (FTC), an estimated 9 million Americans have their identities stolen every year. And the Privacy Rights Clearinghouse says that since 2005, more than 500 million cases of compromised digital information have occurred in database attacks on businesses, governments, institutions, and other organizations. The Privacy Rights Clearinghouse is a nonprofit consumer education and advocacy group in San Diego, California.

Many people victimized by identity theft or fraud do not learn about it until they attempt to carry out a transaction, such as pay their taxes, like these people at the tax office in Fairfax, Virginia.

IT'S A CRIME

Most cybercrimes start with identity theft, also called identity fraud. Identity theft is obtaining personal information to pose as another person without his or her permission. Examples of targeted data include birth dates, driver's license numbers, usernames, passwords, bank account numbers, credit/debit card numbers, Social Security numbers, health care IDs, and more. Identity theft is a crime in itself. So are wrongful uses of the information for the purpose of fraud or deception—usually for financial gain.

SEVEN WAYS IDENTITY THEFT HURTS TEENS

Many of the negative effects of identity theft apply mostly to adults. However, teens are at risk, too. Here are seven ways stolen identification affects young adults.

1. **Attacks on your contacts.** If you have a weak password (or, worse yet, you reveal your password to others), hackers can take over your email and social media accounts. Sometimes, they can send your contacts spam or phishing schemes that look like they came from you.
2. **Entry to other websites.** You likely use your email address as a username on other accounts. Armed with your hacked password, thieves can pose as you on these sites. They may be able to reset your passwords on other accounts and use them for their own gain.
3. **Invasion of privacy.** Hackers who gain control of Facebook, Twitter, or other social media accounts can see everything you and your followers post.
4. **Unauthorized posts.** Posts that look like they come from you can be used for online stalking, actions that you will likely be blamed for.
5. **Cyberbullying.** Again, posing as you, a hacker can intimidate or terrorize others.
6. **Tax refund theft.** Without your knowing it, a criminal can file a false tax return and claim a refund due to you. When you file your real return, you might not get your money.

(continued on the next page)

(continued from the previous page)

7. False arrest. If someone posing as you breaks the law, police can get a warrant for your arrest and throw you in jail—at least temporarily.

If you fall victim to any cybercrimes, report them to local police, the state attorney general, and/or the internet Crime Complaint Center, a partnership between the Federal Bureau of Investigation and the National White Collar Crime Center.

Armed with enough personal information, a criminal can falsely apply for loans and credit cards in the victim's name, withdraw money from bank accounts, use the victim's online accounts, file changes of address, contract for mobile phone service, rent a car, or get goods and privileges the thief could not receive using his or her real name. The victim may be saddled with bills, fees, and a damaged credit score that he or she knows nothing about—until it's too late.

HOW DOES IDENTITY THEFT HAPPEN?

According to the US Department of Justice, the three most common ways identity theft occurs are from using online services in a public place, discarding applications for "preapproved" credit cards, and answering spam, or unsolicited emails.

Using your laptop or phone in public, for example, risks that a criminal will "shoulder surf." Shoulder surfing

Like a lost smartphone, papers discarded carelessly in a refuse bin where anybody can recover them can be an open invitation to identity thieves.

is watching a victim punch in a credit card number—or listening when the victim speaks the information over a phone. Some public places, such as coffee shops, airports, cafés, and hotels, offer wireless internet access for laptops, smartphones, or other devices. These locations are known as Wi-Fi hotspots. They may offer the service free or for a fee. The danger comes if the Wi-Fi network is unsecured. An unsecured network allows the flow of data that can be easily intercepted, especially if the device lacks a security or antimalware product.

Use of an unsecured network gives cyber criminals many opportunities. They can get your login credentials, but they can also intercept, modify, or steal your data, including corporate information, images, media files, and the content of emails and instant messages. They can spread malware to network users. They might also use the network to transmit hate speech or other unsavory content.

YOU'RE PREAPPROVED!

The morning mail includes a letter from a credit card encouraging you to apply or announcing that you're preapproved for one. The first requires an application that will then be run through a credit check to see if you're eligible. The second is more dangerous. All you do is check a box, and the company sends you a card.

The trouble comes if you simply toss the offer in the trash. A criminal digging through your trash bin can retrieve the offer and accept it for himself or herself. If your mailbox is accessible to others, the criminal can simply grab the offer and the subsequently mailed card before you even know it's there. You may not know a thing until you get a bill for purchases you never made. You may be denied a credit card or bank loan because the thief has ruined your credit rating by failing to pay the bills.

SPAM SCAMS

Unsolicited email, called spam, poses additional risks if the user responds to it. Some spam simply wants you as a customer. Some pose potential problems. One is called phishing. You get an email that looks like it comes from a company you do business with. It promises some benefit or asks you to help solve a problem.

One such scam looked like it legitimately came from the Amazon.com shopping service. Since so many people shop there, an email sent to random users is likely to land in an Amazon customer's inbox. The email read, in so many words, "There is a problem identifying your payment

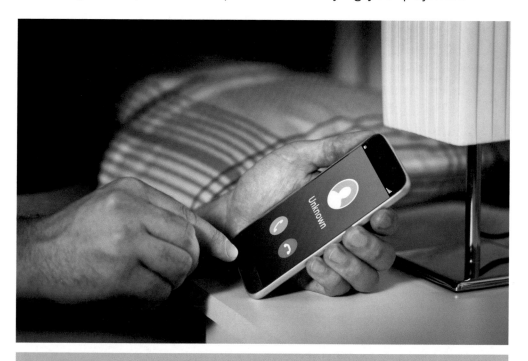

Spam phone calls, many of which are placed by identity thieves and other untrustworthy characters, are a common nuisance for many people nowadays.

method for your recent purchase." The message also included a "convenient" link that, again, looked like it connected to Amazon. There, the user was asked to reenter payment information and other personal data like mailing or shipping addresses.

If you get such an email and think the claim may be correct, you can safely avoid turning over your information to a criminal by refusing to click on the "helpful" link. Instead, use your browser to connect directly to the service's website and investigate further. One user who received this phishing email from "Amazon" went directly to the Amazon website and discovered that the item in question had already shipped, proving there was no issue with his payment method.

Identity theft can also result from a user sharing passwords, unknowingly downloading malware, or using an ATM that a criminal has attached a skimming device to collect people's account numbers and passwords. In other cases, thieves gain access to your personal information as part of a privacy or security breach of business, government, or educational databases.

STAYING SAFE ONLINE

Your personal behavior can go a long way toward protecting your online identity. First, you can limit your screen time. The less time you spend on the web, the less information you add to your identity. Avoid sharing such personal data as your full name, address, or birth date. Keep your social media activity private. If you are tagged in an objectionable photo on social media, it is best to delete it. Also block or delete negative comments on your pages. Tighten privacy settings on social media. Check for privacy choices on websites and enable them. Look for an "https://" prefix and a locked padlock symbol before the web address of any website where you shop or enter personal data.

Beware of links in emails, comments, tweets, posts and elsewhere, especially if you cannot trust the sender. And never try to go to a banking or other financial website by clicking on a link that came in an email, no matter how legitimate it looks. Instead go to

Taking as many precautions as possible to protect your identity and maintain your privacy online will go a long way to establishing digital peace of mind.

your browser and enter your institution's web address to go there directly.

Before using a wireless connection in a Wi-Fi hotspot, verify that you're using the correct one. Some cyber criminals create connections similar to the ones offered by the coffee shop, hotel, etc., that you're using.

OPEN SESAME

Even though passwords hold the key to personal information, many people are careless when choosing and using them. In fact, in a study released in 2016, Leaked-Source, a service with a database of security breaches, listed the most common passwords used by members of the LinkedIn professional network. With 753,305 users, the most popular password was "123456." The next two most used passwords on the network were "linkedin" with 172,523 users and "password," used by 144,458. In fourth and fifth places, respectively, were 123456789 (94,314 users) and 12345678 (63,769 users).

A strong password should have at least sixteen characters. Include at least one uppercase letter, a lowercase letter, a number, and a symbol. Avoid such commonly available information as the names of family members or pets, house or phone numbers, birth dates, or Social Security numbers.

Use a different password and security question for each site and don't let your web browser store your passwords. Change your passwords every ten to twelve weeks. And, of course, never share your password with anyone, especially in a text or email.

Check with an employee to get the correct connection name and IP address.

DEVICE ADVICE

Keep all your technology devices updated. Often, updates include fixes for software glitches that are open to attack. Be sure that all your mobile devices are protected by a password, biometrics, or other security. Turn off any file-sharing options on your devices to prevent identity thieves from gaining access to your public folders. And, limit the information you store in these folders.

Instead of using a public Wi-Fi connection when you're shopping or need to transfer money between bank accounts, use your protected mobile phone network. And, of course, be sure all your devices are using a current version of security software from such companies as McAfee, Norton, or Webroot. Nothing stored electronically is 100 percent safe from cyber criminals. But if you take these steps, you'll minimize the risk that your identity will be stolen and used for illegal purposes.

ACTIVITIES

Build a Digital Identity . . . from Scratch!

A group of several students, or several groups in a class-room working separately in a friendly competitive spirit, design a digital identity from scratch, using a fake perso-na—for example, called Person A.

Each team or individual, depending on how the group work is divided in a classroom or among a smaller group of students, handles a different aspect of Person A's online identity. Individual teams can:

- Set up an email address for Person A, establishing privacy settings, contacts, etc.
- Sign up Person A for mailing lists, other accounts and services, using his or her email address.
- Set up different social media accounts for Person A, including Facebook, Instagram, Twitter, and others. All team members (and groups, if the project encompass-es a whole classroom) can friend or add Person A and act as if Person A is an actual individual.
- Different teams can be in charge of different aspects of Person A's activity. For example, one group might try to improve A's digital identity with solely positive posts, comments, and online activity, while another might attempt to derail these. Note: Any "negative" activity should not rise to the level of harassment, bullying, or lawbreaking of any kind.
- Person A can become a job seeker and place mock résumés on a personal site, blog, or in other

online spaces, including on job sites like Indeed, HotJobs, etc.

- Students can brainstorm other aspects of digital identity that Person A might help them explore.
- The project can extend over a week or more and may take on a life of its own. The supervision of a trusted adult—most likely a teacher—will be necessary to ensure that the project stays on course and adheres to applicable rules, laws, and ethical standards.

Activity 2
Digital Identity: Then and Now

Students divide into teams/groups to explore, via research and interviews, how digital identity has changed over time, how it works today, and how it may transform in the near and distant future.

- Email or interview parents, grandparents, and other trusted adults about what kinds of identification they were used to, and collect mini oral histories about what the older generations carried in their wallets, and how they engaged in banking and other administrative tasks before the online era.
- Ask the same trusted, older adults for permission to perform internet searches on them, and compare/contrast their online presence(s) to those of modern teens. Are there commonalities? Are some of the sample adults more internet savvy than others?
- If any of the adults queried hail from different nations and cultures, find out and write up short reports on how standards of digital identity might differ in those cultures.

- Students can craft visual presentations by scanning or photographing old copies of documents and identification papers once used widely but now replaced with modern versions, and by comparing and contrasting the benefits and drawbacks of both eras.

Activity 3
Digital identity Cards

Individuals or groups can play against each other using a standard deck of playing cards, or improvised ones, and a set of dice. The aim of the game is to build up a good digital identity by collecting all the cards representing positive building blocks, and attempting to discard or pass along any negative aspects.

- Cards in play might represent things like: emailed hacked/identity stolen > -5 points; compromising pictures detected > -2 points; harassing posts or comments recorded > -2 points;. . . and so forth.
- Initiate the game by having each player roll the dice and take the indicated number of cards from the deck. After players receive their hand, they take turns going around the circle, rolling the dice to decide whether they can discard negative cards and take positive ones from the pile. Players agree on a set number of rounds, declaring the winner with the best cards.

GLOSSARY

behavioral advertising A type of marketing based on information about consumers collected from web browsing behavior. Also called behavioral targeting.

best practices Guidelines that have become accepted standards of operation for members of an industry.

biometrics The measurement and analysis of a person's unique physical and behavioral traits.

Bitcoin A worldwide payment system using electronic cash that allows encrypted electronic payments from one party to another without the need for a bank or other financial institution.

blog A frequently updated website or webpage where individuals (and businesses) provide something of interest on the internet.

blogosphere The total of all blogs and personal websites on the internet.

cookie A permanent or temporary text file containing personal and behavioral information sent by a website's web server to a web browser on the user's computer to let the website "recognize" a user and track his or her choices.

cryptographic hashing The process of transforming a string of characters into a shorter, coded message.

data breach An intentional or unintentional incident in which confidential information is released, viewed, or stolen by an unauthorized entity.

data shadow A slang term for the total of all traces of someone's online activities.

digital dirt Any unflattering photos or information connected to your name online that contributes to a negative online reputation.

digital identity The sum of information about a person or company that is available online.

digital portfolio An electronic collection of information that demonstrates academic achievements over time.

identity theft Obtaining personal information to pose as another person without his or her permission.

multifactor authentication (MFA) An online security method that requires two or more pieces of information at login.

personal brand A consistent, truthful way to present yourself to others—both online and offline.

personal learning network A group of people a person chooses to interact with for the purpose of exchanging ideas, questions, thoughts, and resources.

proof of concept Documented evidence that a product or service can be successful in a real-world environment.

quick response (QR) code A machine-readable barcode consisting of a two-dimensional arrangement of black and white squares that stores encoded data.

shoulder surfing Watching a potential identity-theft victim punch in a credit card number in a public place, or listening when the victim speaks the information over a phone.

Wi-Fi hotspot A public place, such as a coffee shop, airport, café, or hotel, that offers wireless internet access for laptops, smartphones, or other devices.

FOR MORE INFORMATION

Center for Internet Security (CIS)
31 Tech Valley Drive, Suite 2
East Greenbush, NY 12061
(518) 266-3460
Website: https://www.cisecurity.org
Facebook: @CenterforIntSec
Twitter: @CISecurity
CIS is a nonprofit organization that focuses on cyber
    threat prevention, response, and recovery to pro-
    tect data.

Digital Media Academy
1550 Dell Avenue, Suite C
Campbell, CA 95008
(866) 656-3342
Website: https://www.digitalmediaacademy.org
Facebook: @digitalmediaacademy.org
Twitter: @DMA_org
Located at seventeen campuses in the United States
    and Canada, these camps for kids and teens include
    choices of programming, game design, and more.

iDTech
910 E. Hamilton Avenue, Suite 300
Campbell, CA 95008
(888) 709-8324
Website: https://www.idtech.com
Facebook: @computercamps
Twitter: @iDTechCamps

With locations in thirty states, as well as Singapore, Hong Kong, and the United Kingdom, iDTech offers multiple digital camp experiences for all ages.

i-SAFE Inc.
6189 El Camino Real, Suite 201
Carlsbad, CA 92009
(760) 603-7911
Website: http://www.isafe.org
Facebook: @isafe.org
Twitter: @iSAFEVentures
I-SAFE Inc. is the nonprofit arm of i-SAFE Ventures. It provides multimedia educational programming for students in grades kindergarten through twelve.

Junior Coders Learning Center
1-2021 Williams Parkway, Unit 1
Brampton, ON L6S 5P4
Canada
(416) 613-1278
Email: info@juniorcoders.ca
Website: http://juniorcoders.ca
Facebook: @juniorcoders.ca
Twitter: @juniorcoders
This center lets students in grades one through twelve learn computer science and programming working together in a friendly environment.

National Cybersecurity Student Association
Prince George's Community College
Center for Advance Technology (CAT), Room CAT129C

301 Largo Road
Largo, MD 20774
(301) 546-0760
Website: http://www.cyberstudents.org
Facebook: @cyberstudents.org
Twitter: @cyberstudents.org
The National Cybersecurity Student Association works
    to strengthen students' education in preparation for
    a career in cybersecurity. It provides activities, net-
    working, and scholarship opportunities.

Technology Student Association
1904 Association Drive
Reston, VA 20191-1540
(888) 860-9010
Website: http://www.tsaweb.org
Facebook and Twitter: @nationalTSA
The Technology Student Association offers opportuni-
    ties to strengthen personal development, leadership,
    and career opportunities through competitions and
    intra-curricular programs.

Tomorrow's Master of Digital Media Program
685 Great Northern Way
Vancouver, BC V5T 0C6
Canada
(855) 737-2666
Email: admin@thecdm.ca
Website: https://thecdm.ca
Facebook: @CentreforDigitalMedia
Twitter: @CentreDigiMedia

This two-week camp for students entering grades nine through twelve lets campers explore educational and career opportunities in the games and digital media industry while building a playable product.

Youth Digital Camps
PO Box 51309
Durham, NC 27707
Email: info@youthdigital.com
Website: http://www.youthdigitalcamps.com
These camps in nine states for kids ages eight to fourteen offer project-based STEM courses developed by designers, programmers, and teachers.

FOR FURTHER READING

Baym, Nancy K. *Personal Connections in the Digital Age* (Digital Media and Society). Cambridge, UK: Polity Press, 2015.

Bernard, Romily. *Find Me.* New York, NY: HarperTeen, 2014.

Boyd, Danah. *It's Complicated: The Social Lives of Networked Teens.* New Haven, CT: Yale University Press, 2015.

Cover, Rob. *Digital Identities: Creating and Communicating the Online Self.* Waltham, MA: Academic Press, 2016.

Gardner, Howard, and Katie Davis. *The App Generation: How Today's Youth Navigate Identity, Intimacy, and Imagination in a Digital World.* New Haven, CT: Yale University Press 2014.

Goodman, Marc. *Future Crimes.* New York, NY: Doubleday, 2015.

Kidd, Dustin. *Social Media Freaks: Digital Identity in the Network Society.* Abingdon, UK: Routledge, 2017.

LeClair, Jane, and Gregory Keeley. *Cybersecurity in Our Digital Lives* (Protecting Our Future). Albany, NY: Hudson Whitman Excelsior College Press, 2015.

Meeuwisse, Raef. *Cybersecurity for Beginners.* Canterbury, UK: Lulu Publishing, 2015.

Selby, Nick, and Heather Vescent. *Cyber Attack Survival Manual: From Identity Theft to the Digital Apocalypse and Everything in Between.* San Francisco, CA: Weldon Books, 2017.

BIBLIOGRAPHY

Cobb, Stephen. "Data Privacy and Data Protection: US Law and Legislation White Paper." WeLiveSecurity.com, April 26, 2016. https://www.welivesecurity.com/2016/04/26/data -privacy-data-protection-us-law-legislation-white -paper.

Desforges, Roxanne. "Crafting Your Digital Identity: The Basics." LearningBird.com. Retrieved January 12, 2018. https://blog.learningbird.com/crafting-your -digital-identity-the-basics.

DLAPiperDataProtection.com. "Data Protection Laws of the World." January 25, 2017. https://www.dlapiperdataprotection.com /index.html?c=US&c2=&t=law.

Erskine, Ryan. "How to Define Your Personal Brand in 5 Simple Steps." Entrepreneur.com, July 7, 2016. https://www.entrepreneur.com/article/278480.

Gemalto.com. "Digital Driver's License: Your ID in Your Smartphone." January 11, 2018. https://www .gemalto.com/govt/traffic/digital-driver-license.

Harvard Law Review. "Riley v. California." Retrieved March 29, 2018. https://harvardlawreview.org/2014/11 /riley-v-california.

Haughn, Matthew, and David Strom. "FIDO (Fast Identity Online)." WhatIs.com, February 2018. http://searchsecurity.techtarget.com/definition /FIDO-Fast-Identity-Online.

Kolk, Melinda. "Building Digital Portfolios." Creative Educator. Retrieved August 15, 2017.

http://creativeeducator.tech4learning.com/v05/articles
/Digital_Portfolios.

Lake, Laura "Personal Branding and What You Need
to Know About It." TheBalance.com, February 19,
2018. https://www.thebalance.com/what-is-personal
-branding-4056073.

Loshin, Peter, and Michael Cobb. "Biometrics."
SearchSecurity/Tech Target, December 2017. http:
//searchsecurity.techtarget.com/definition/biometrics.

Mearian, Lucas. "What Is Blockchain? The Most
Disruptive Tech in Decades." *Computer World*,
January 18, 2018. https://www.computerworld.
com/article/3191077/security/what-is
-blockchain-the-most-disruptive-tech-in
-decades.html.

Mears, Chance. "Why Organizations Need Adaptive
Multi-factor Authentication (MFA)." Centrify Perspective,
December 21, 2016. https://blog.centrify.com
/adaptive-multi-factor-authentication-mfa.

Rahman, Zara. "Digital Identification Systems:
Responsible Data Challenges and Opportunities."
The Engine Room, July 4, 2017. https://www
.theengineroom.org/digital-identification-systems.

Rubenking. Neil J. "5 Ways Identity Theft Can Ruin Your
Life." *PC Mag*, November 19, 2014. https://www
.pcmag.com/article2/0,2817,2472346,00.asp.

Sweetwood, Matt. "7 Social Media Power Techniques
That Build Your Brand and Business." *Entrepreneur*,
December 17, 2015. https://www.entrepreneur.com
/article/254043.

Sweetwood, Matt. "8 Reasons a Powerful Personal Brand Will Make You Successful." *Entrepreneur*, March 27, 2017. https://www.entrepreneur.com /article/289278.

Threat Metrix. *The Definitive Guide to Digital Identity.* 2018. https://www.digitalidentityguide.com/the -network-effect.

Weishaar, Paige. "8 Steps to Creating a Digital Identity." Infogram.com. Retrieved January 12, 2018. https://infogram.com/8-steps-to-creating-a-digital -identity-1g0q3pl30ro6p1g.

Wladawsky-Berger, Irving. "Digital Identity: The Key to Privacy and Security in the Digital World." *MIT Digital*, August 29, 2016. http://ide.mit.edu /news-blog/blog/digital-identity-key-privacy-and -security-digital-world.

WomenForHire.com. "Create Your Digital Identity." Retrieved January 12, 2018. http://womenforhire .com/beginning_your_job_search/create_your _digital_identity.

INDEX

ABOUT THE AUTHOR

Mary-Lane Kamberg is a professional writer and author and has published the following internet-related titles for Rosen Publishing: *Cybersecurity: Protecting Your Identity and Data*, *Becoming a Database Administrator*, *Becoming a Systems Administrator*, and *Getting a Job in the IT Industry*. She also wrote extensively for *Transaction Trends*, a trade magazine for the credit and debit card industry. She lives in Olathe, Kansas, and is founder and director of the I Love to Write Summer Camp for young writers.

PHOTO CREDITS

Cover Hero Images/Getty Images; cover, back cover, and interior pages background (abstract) Toria/Shutterstock.com; cover, p. 3 (icons) pluie_r/Shutterstock.com; p. 5 Jan H Andersen/Shutterstock.com; p. 8 Plamen Resseleshki/iStock/Thinkstock; p. 10 Dean Mouhtaropoulos /Getty Images; p. 14 Andrey_Popov/Shutterstock.com; p. 17 zimmytws /Shutterstock.com; p. 20 Chinnapong/Shutterstock.com; p. 22 Splash News/Alamy Stock Photo; p. 23 PixieMe/Shutterstock.com; p. 25 Charlotte Purdy/Shutterstock.com; p. 28 Asia Images Group/Shutterstock.com; p. 33 wavebreakmedia/Shutterstock.com; p. 36 mama_mia/Shutterstock .com; p. 38 JMiks/Shutterstock.com; p. 40 © AP Images; p. 43 Benny Marty/Shutterstock.com; p. 45 Saul Loeb/AFP/Getty Images; p. 50 Jeremy Woodhouse/Blend Images/Thinkstock; p. 51 encierro/Shutterstock.com; p. 54 Chip Somodevilla/Getty Images; p. 57 Ralf Geithe/Shutterstock .com; p. 59 Tero Vesalainen/Shutterstock.com; p. 61 tommaso79/iStock /Thinkstock.

Design: Michael Moy; Editor: Philip Wolny; Photo Researcher: Nicole DiMella